The Word
of
My Patience

Dag Heward-Mills

Parchment House

THE WORD OF MY PATIENCE

Copyright © 2022 Dag Heward-Mills

Published by Parchment House 2022
1st Printing 2022

[77]Find out more about Dag Heward-Mills
Healing Jesus Campaign
Write to: evangelist@daghewardmills.org
Website: www.daghewardmills.org
Facebook: Dag Heward-Mills
Twitter: @EvangelistDag

ISBN: 978-1-64330-512-7

Contents

CHAPTER 1

"The Word of My Patience"

Because thou hast kept THE WORD OF MY PATIENCE, I also will keep thee from the hour of temptation, which shall come upon all the world, to try them that dwell upon the earth.

Revelation 3:10

"The Word of my patience" is a "Word that requires patience". Patience for what? Patience is required in order for this Word to be fulfilled or to come to pass. Anything that God says that requires patience is a "Word of my patience". Most of the promises of God are examples of "the Word of my patience". God promises many things in the Bible. God promises many good things and good changes for our lives. Most of these promises need patience to be fulfilled.

One of the common examples of a "Word of my patience" is the call of God. God's call to your life is something that requires patience if it is to be fulfilled. It could take years for the call of God to be fulfilled. Sometimes it takes centuries for the call of God to be fulfilled.

"The Word of my patience" is a Word that requires you to endure much provocation, annoyance or pain without complaint. "The Word of my patience" is a Word that requires you to endure tests and temptations and misfortune without losing your temper or becoming irritated.

"The Word of my patience" requires a steady, quiet perseverance and diligence if you are to ever see the manifestation of the promise of God.

It is nice to hear of the call of God. It is wonderful to see that God has called you. It is wonderful to hear of the great things that God has promised to do through you, by you and with you. However, you must expect to go through many things before you see the manifestation of God's power in your life.

"The Word of my patience" requires calmness.

"The Word of my patience" is the call of God and it requires composure and calmness.

"The Word of my patience" requires constancy, diligence and endurance.

"The Word of my patience" requires forbearance and fortitude.

"The Word of my patience" requires self-control and serenity.

"The Word of my patience" requires tolerance, persistence and perseverance.

Dear friend, in fulfilling the will of God and surging forward to experience "the Word of my patience" you must accept that you will go through many things which you must accept with calmness, forbearance and fortitude.

I met a young man who was disgruntled and discontented because he had been in the ministry for five years and had nothing to show for it. Many pastors are disappointed and disillusioned. However, they would not be disappointed and disillusioned if they would consider their own role in bringing themselves to the place of disappointment and disillusionment.

"The Word of my patience" is the call of God. The call of God requires you to grow in honesty in your own self-assessment. It is only after many years that you will have an accurate and humble assessment of yourself.

Apostle Paul calls himself someone who does not come behind the chiefest of the apostles. "For I suppose I was not a whit behind the very chiefest apostles" (2 Corinthians 11:5). However, he grew in his assessment of himself and said he was the least of the apostles (1 Corinthians 15:9). In the end, Paul simply called himself the chief of sinners (1 Timothy 1:15).

Some time ago, I sat in front of an erratic young man who was leaving the church. He had been brought up in the church, since his youth. He had been looked after, cared for, guided and counselled for many years. Suddenly, he was abandoning his church and the pastors he had known for many years. Why? Because he was offended about something minor.

As I looked at him, I figured out that he did not have the right estimation of himself and of how much he was at fault in his own life. Because he did not have the patience, the fortitude and the stamina, he was losing out on the future that he would have had in the ministry.

Patience is the "good-natured tolerance of delay". Many young people do not have the tolerance to endure delays and inactivity.

Many things have to be put off till later because you are not ready for them. Most people are irritated when they have to put off their rewards till later. Some people cannot stand it when you rebuke them. Patience involves enduring many rebukes, many corrections and many unpleasant meetings. Are you ready to go through these things until you begin to bear the kind of fruit you saw in your visions and dreams?

One of the things that happens when you are developing in "the Word of my patience" is that you grow in a wise and true estimation of yourself and how wrong you are, how weak you are, how problematic you are and how much grace you need.

It takes time, endurance and strength of character to go through the different phases of life and ministry until you are bearing the kind of fruit you saw in the dreams and visions of God. The dreams and visions of God are His "Word of my patience" to you.

God loves you! But He will not lower His standards for you. If Jesus went through hardships that require patience, meekness and forgiveness, you will also go through hardships which require patience, meekness and forgiveness.

The call of God is without repentance. What God said will surely come to pass. Though it tarry, wait for it for it will surely come.

For the vision is yet for an appointed time, but at the end it shall speak, and not lie: though it tarry, wait for it; because it will surely come, it will not tarry.

Habakkuk 2:3

God is going to use you mightily: that is an example of a "Word of my patience".

You are going to become a great man of God: that is another "Word of my patience".

Your latter end will greatly increase: that is a "Word of my patience".

You are going to have a mega church: that is a "Word of my patience".

One day, you will travel all over the world to serve the Lord: that is a "Word of my patience".

I see you having great crusades and winning souls: that is a "Word of my patience".

You will walk in the same anointing that I am carrying: that is a "Word of my patience".

You will last: that is a "Word of my patience".

You will survive: that is a "Word of my patience".

A thousand will fall at your side and ten thousand at your right hand: that is a "Word of my patience".

A righteous man falleth seven times but rises again: that is a "Word of my patience".

You will have a good marriage: that is a "Word of my patience".

Two are better than one so your life is going to be better from today: that is a "Word of my patience".

One shall put to flight a thousand but two shall put to flight ten thousand: that is a "Word of my patience".

When a man has found a wife, he has found a good thing and obtained favour with God. You have found a good thing and you have obtained favour with God: that is a "Word of my patience".

All these statements are prophecies! They are all examples of "the Word of my patience". With time, with patience, with fortitude, with calmness, with composure, with tolerance and endurance, you will see every single one of these prophecies come to pass in your life.

CHAPTER 2

"The Word of My Patience" For Abraham: Twenty-Five Years

Now the Lord had said unto Abram, Get thee out of thy country, and from thy kindred, and from thy father's house, unto a land that I will shew thee: And I will make of thee a great nation, and I will bless thee, and make thy name great; and thou shalt be a blessing: And I will bless them that bless thee, and curse him that curseth thee: and in thee shall all families of the earth be blessed. SO ABRAM DEPARTED, AS THE LORD HAD SPOKEN UNTO HIM; AND LOT WENT WITH HIM: AND ABRAM WAS SEVENTY AND FIVE YEARS OLD WHEN HE DEPARTED OUT OF HARAN.

Genesis 12:1-4

1. Abraham was called by God at the age of seventy-five. At that point God told him that he was going to become a great nation. He received the call of God in which he was blessed to become a blessing. Everyone who blessed Abraham would be blessed and everyone who cursed Abraham would be cursed.

    Now the Lord had said unto Abram, Get thee out of thy country, and from thy kindred, and from thy father's house, unto a land that I will shew thee: And I will make of thee a great nation, and I will bless thee, and make thy name great; and thou shalt be a blessing: And I will bless them that bless thee, and curse him that curseth thee: and in thee shall all families of the earth be blessed. SO ABRAM DEPARTED, AS THE LORD HAD SPOKEN UNTO HIM; AND LOT WENT WITH HIM: AND ABRAM WAS SEVENTY AND FIVE YEARS OLD WHEN HE DEPARTED OUT OF HARAN.

    Genesis 12:1-4

2. Abraham received yet another "Word of my patience" when he was ninety years old. At this stage he was given a call of God in which there would be great multiplication. Today, many people have received the call of God and the promise of God for great multiplication. Many people have heard from the Holy Spirit that He would increase them and multiply them greatly. This is a "Word of my patience". It is important to recognize that the call of God and the promise of God for multiplication always requires patience.

    AND WHEN ABRAM WAS NINETY YEARS OLD AND NINE, THE LORD APPEARED TO ABRAM, AND SAID UNTO HIM, I AM THE ALMIGHTY GOD; WALK BEFORE ME, AND BE THOU PERFECT. AND I WILL MAKE MY COVENANT BETWEEN ME AND THEE, AND WILL MULTIPLY THEE EXCEEDINGLY. And Abram fell on his face: and God talked with him, saying, As for me, behold, my covenant is with thee, and thou shalt be a father of many nations. Neither shall thy

8

name any more be called Abram, but thy name shall be Abraham; for a father of many nations have I made thee. And I will make thee exceeding fruitful, and I will make nations of thee, and kings shall come out of thee. And I will establish my covenant between me and thee and thy seed after thee in their generations for an everlasting covenant, to be a God unto thee, and to thy seed after thee. And I will give unto thee, and to thy seed after thee, the land wherein thou art a stranger, all the land of Canaan, for an everlasting possession; and I will be their God.

Genesis 17:1-8

3. Twenty-five years after receiving the first call of God, Abraham began to see signs that he could become what God had told him he would become. Remember that Abraham was seventy-five years old when God told him to move away from his family so that He could bless him. Abraham was a hundred years old when his son, Isaac, was born.

And the Lord visited Sarah as he had said, and the LORD did unto Sarah as he had spoken. For Sarah conceived, and bare Abraham a son in his old age, at the set time of which God had spoken to him. And Abraham called the name of his son that was born unto him, whom Sarah bare to him, Isaac. AND ABRAHAM CIRCUMCISED HIS SON ISAAC BEING EIGHT DAYS OLD, AS GOD HAD COMMANDED HIM. AND ABRAHAM WAS AN HUNDRED YEARS OLD, WHEN HIS SON ISAAC WAS BORN UNTO HIM.

Genesis 21:1-5

CHAPTER 3

"The Word of My Patience" For Jacob

And Jacob went out from Beersheba, and went toward Haran. And he lighted upon a certain place, and tarried there all night, because the sun was set; and he took of the stones of that place, and put them for his pillows, and lay down in that place to sleep.

And he dreamed, and behold a ladder set up on the earth, and the top of it reached to heaven: and behold the angels of God ascending and descending on it.

And, behold, the Lord stood above it, and said, I am the Lord God of Abraham thy father, and the God of Isaac: THE LAND WHEREON THOU LIEST, TO THEE WILL I GIVE IT, AND TO THY SEED; AND THY SEED SHALL BE AS THE DUST OF THE EARTH, AND THOU SHALT SPREAD ABROAD TO THE WEST, AND TO THE EAST, AND TO THE NORTH, AND TO THE SOUTH: AND IN THEE AND IN THY SEED SHALL ALL THE FAMILIES OF THE EARTH BE BLESSED. AND, BEHOLD, I AM WITH THEE, AND WILL

KEEP THEE IN ALL PLACES WHITHER THOU GOEST, AND WILL BRING THEE AGAIN INTO THIS LAND; FOR I WILL NOT LEAVE THEE, UNTIL I HAVE DONE THAT WHICH I HAVE SPOKEN TO THEE OF. And Jacob awaked out of his sleep, and he said, surely the Lord is in this place; and I knew it not.

Genesis 28:10-16

Jacob was called by God and given a great promise, "Your seed will be like the dust of the earth. You will spread from the west to the east, to the north and to the south."

Even though this blessing was promised to Jacob, it was a Word that would take many years to be fulfilled. A number of seasons were about to begin in the life of Jacob. The first two seasons were made up of seven years each.

To be given mighty promises is not enough. You need to understand that the call of God will not just fall on you like ripe mangoes falling off a tree. You will need to exercise patience and go through long periods of emptiness where you trust that God will lift you up. If Jacob had not had patience, he would never have become Israel.

1. **The first season of Jacob's life that required patience was the seven years in which he was ostensibly paying for Rachel, but ended up with Leah. Jacob had to endure being cheated over and over again.**

   AND JACOB LOVED RACHEL; AND SAID, I WILL SERVE THEE SEVEN YEARS FOR RACHEL THY YOUNGER daughter. And Laban said, It is better that I give her to thee, than that I should give her to another man: abide with me. And Jacob served seven years for Rachel; and they seemed unto him but a few days, for the love he had to her.

   Genesis 29:18-20

2. **The second season of Jacob's life which required patience lasted seven years in which he was paying for Rachel, the daughter of Laban.**

   FULFIL HER WEEK, AND WE WILL GIVE THEE THIS ALSO FOR THE SERVICE WHICH THOU SHALT SERVE WITH ME YET SEVEN OTHER YEARS. And Jacob did so, and fulfilled her week: and he gave him Rachel his daughter to wife also.

   Genesis 29:27-28

3. **The third season of Jacob's life was where he spent six years paying for some of the cattle of Laban.**

    THUS HAVE I BEEN TWENTY YEARS IN THY HOUSE; I SERVED THEE FOURTEEN YEARS FOR THY TWO DAUGHTERS, AND SIX YEARS FOR THY CATTLE: and thou hast changed my wages ten times. Except the God of my father, the God of Abraham, and the fear of Isaac, had been with me, surely thou hadst sent me away now empty. God hath seen mine affliction and the labour of my hands, and rebuked thee yesternight.

    Genesis 31:41-42

4. **The next season of Jacob's life was spent bringing up rebellious children who abducted, kidnapped and "murdered" their own brother, Joseph.**

    How could God's perfect will and promises come to pass through such wicked and heartless children? Indeed, it is a "Word of my patience"! Jacob lived a long life and when he met Pharaoh, he was 147 years old. When Jacob finally met up with Pharaoh, he told Pharaoh that he had experienced a lot of evil in his life. You will need patience to go through the amount of treachery and evil that Jacob endured in his lifetime. There is no calling that goes unopposed. The call of God is real but there are a lot of adversaries. These adversaries are going to make sure that you slow down and if possible, quit.

    AND JACOB SAID UNTO PHARAOH, THE DAYS OF THE YEARS OF MY PILGRIMAGE ARE AN HUNDRED AND THIRTY YEARS: few and evil have the days of the years of my life been, and have not attained unto the days of the years of the life of my fathers in the days of their pilgrimage.

    Genesis 47:9

    And Jacob lived in the land of Egypt seventeen years: so the whole age of Jacob was an hundred forty and seven years.

    Genesis 47:28

13

CHAPTER 4

"The Word of My Patience" For Joseph

And JOSEPH DREAMED A DREAM, and he told it his brethren: and they hated him yet the more. And he said unto them, Hear, I pray you, this dream which I have dreamed:

For, behold, we were binding sheaves in the field, and, lo, my sheaf arose, and also stood upright; and, behold, your sheaves stood round about, and made obeisance to my sheaf. And his brethren said to him, SHALT THOU INDEED REIGN OVER US? OR SHALT THOU INDEED HAVE DOMINION OVER US? And they hated him yet the more for his dreams, and for his words.

AND HE DREAMED YET ANOTHER DREAM, and told it his brethren, and said, Behold, I have dreamed a dream more; and, behold, the sun and the moon and the eleven stars made obeisance to me. And he told it to his father, and to his brethren: and his father rebuked him, and said unto him, what is this dream that thou hast dreamed? SHALL I AND THY MOTHER AND THY BRETHREN INDEED COME TO BOW DOWN OURSELVES TO THEE TO THE EARTH?

Genesis 37:5-10

Your life is just like the life of Joseph. God called him when he was a child. His childhood dreams were clearly prophetic in nature. God had great things in store for him. God was going to make him great and even his parents and his brothers, would one day, come and bow before him.

But all these dreams were not going to come to pass until Joseph learnt what patience was about.

The dreams of God are real. Make no mistake about it! God is real! His visions and dreams are real! God does have great things in store. As the scripture says, "I have given you the word of my patience" (Revelations 3:10); that is to say, I have you given you a Word that requires a lot of patience, if you are to see its fulfillment.

Stop planning to have a short and quick ministry with high-speed fulfillment of the fantastic promises of God! Your calling is going to take your whole life. That is why God wants you to start with Him when you are very young. Waiting to serve God when you are on retirement is not the right thing to do. Give yourself when you are young and fresh. Joseph started his ministry by walking in righteousness and honoring his father at the age of seventeen.

> These are the generations of Jacob. JOSEPH, BEING SEVENTEEN YEARS OLD, was feeding the flock with his brethren; and the lad was with the sons of Bilhah, and with the sons of Zilpah, his father's wives: and Joseph brought unto his father their evil report.
>
> Genesis 37:2

Joseph, apparently served in Potiphar's house as a slave for one year and then was in prison for twelve years. These thirteen years were spent waiting for the fulfillment of the dream. From the age of thirty to the age of one hundred and ten, he spent his life fulfilling the visions and dreams God had given to him as a child.

And Joseph was THIRTY YEARS OLD when he stood before Pharaoh king of Egypt. And Joseph went out from the presence of Pharaoh, and went throughout all the land of Egypt.

Genesis 41:46

Joseph was about to go through false accusation, imprisonment, embarrassment and humiliation. Joseph was going to need grace to go through all that God had ordained for him. Finally, he died at the age of a hundred and ten. Joseph had served God since he was seventeen years old.

And Joseph dwelt in Egypt, he, and his father's house: and Joseph lived AN HUNDRED AND TEN YEARS.

Genesis 50:22

CHAPTER 5

"The Word of My Patience" For Moses: Forty Years

And Moses was learned in all the wisdom of the Egyptians, and was mighty in words and in deeds. And WHEN HE WAS FULL FORTY YEARS OLD, IT CAME INTO HIS HEART TO VISIT HIS BRETHREN the children of Israel. And seeing one of them suffer wrong, he defended him, and avenged him that was oppressed, and smote the Egyptian: For he supposed his brethren would have understood how that God by his hand would deliver them: but they understood not.

Acts 7:22-25

G od's call to Moses was another example of "the Word of my patience". "The Word of my patience" requires time, endurance, calmness, tolerance and persistence to accomplish anything. You are going to need patience in order to fulfil the call of God.

1. Moses was forty years old when his heart was stirred up to care for the people of God.

Perhaps your heart is stirred up to care for the people of God. To be stirred up to care for the people of God is to receive the call of God.

And Moses was learned in all the wisdom of the Egyptians, and was mighty in words and in deeds. And WHEN HE WAS FULL FORTY YEARS OLD, IT CAME INTO HIS HEART TO VISIT HIS BRETHREN the children of Israel. And seeing one of them suffer wrong, he defended him, and avenged him that was oppressed, and smote the Egyptian: For he supposed his brethren would have understood how that God by his hand would deliver them: but they understood not.

Acts 7:22-25

2. Moses was eighty years old when God appeared to him in a burning bush and spoke to him.

It took forty years for the stirrings of God to turn into something more substantial. It is important that you do not downplay the amount of time that is needed to grow into the will of God for you. God has great plans for you. Indeed, God has a series of visitations that He has planned for you. He will lead you gently and teach you gradually, all that you need to know. God did not see the need to hurry Moses' calling. He could have appeared to him earlier but He allowed forty years to go by. He allowed Moses to live in the wilderness so that Moses would develop the humility and wisdom that was needed to lead God's people one day.

But he that did his neighbour wrong thrust him away, saying, who made thee a ruler and a judge over us? Wilt thou kill me, as thou diddest the Egyptian yesterday? Then fled Moses at this saying, and was a stranger in the land of Madian, where he begat two sons. And WHEN FORTY YEARS WERE EXPIRED, THERE APPEARED TO HIM IN THE WILDERNESS OF MOUNT SINA AN ANGEL OF THE LORD IN A FLAME OF FIRE IN A BUSH. When Moses saw it, he wondered at the sight: and as he drew near to behold it, the voice of the Lord came unto him,

Acts 7:27-31

3. Moses was eighty years old when he met with Pharaoh.

So Moses and Aaron did it; as the Lord commanded them, thus they did. MOSES WAS EIGHTY YEARS OLD and Aaron eighty-three, when they spoke to Pharaoh.

Exodus 7:6-7 (NASB)

Things started to gallop after the burning bush experience. Moses was catapulted into the forefront of ministry. After forty years of suffering in the wilderness and after the short meeting and encounter with God at the burning bush, Moses was ready for public ministry.

4. Moses was one hundred and twenty years old when he died.

And the Lord's anger was kindled against Israel, and he made them WANDER IN THE WILDERNESS FORTY YEARS, until all the generation, that had done evil in the sight of the LORD, was consumed.

Numbers 32:13

Moses wandered in the wilderness for forty years of his ministry. His ministry was to lead the children of Israel out of Egypt and into The Promised Land.

He was God's great prophet who had received a definite calling at the burning bush. This was "the Word of my patience". By the time Moses was ready to die, another forty years had gone by. Therefore, Moses ministered for forty years before he was able to accomplish part of his ministry. Indeed, he did not even finish his ministry after forty years of struggling in the wilderness.

I do not know the kind of calling you have but I can tell you that it has the characteristics of "the Word of my patience". The call of God needs time, patience, forbearance, tolerance, endurance and longsuffering in order to accomplish it. Do not be unhappy because you have not achieved much in three years. The call of God is "the Word of my patience". It takes many years to accomplish the will of God.

CHAPTER 6

"The Word of My Patience" For Levites: Twenty-five Years

This is it that belongeth unto the Levites: from TWENTY AND FIVE YEARS OLD and upward they shall go in to wait upon the service of the tabernacle of the congregation: And from the age of FIFTY YEARS they shall cease waiting upon the service thereof, and shall serve no more:

Numbers 8:24-25

"The Word of my patience" is the call of God. The call of God will take several years to be fulfilled. I believe that the call of God takes an average of thirty years to be fulfilled.

It is because the call of God requires so many years of dedicated service to accomplish anything that you need patience. This is why the call of God is called "the Word of my patience". If you want to be a Levite you need at least twenty-five years to accomplish anything substantial.

Let us now see how the call of God panned out in the lives of God's servants in the Old Testament.

1. **"The Word of my patience" takes twenty years because the Levites were to minister between the ages of thirty and fifty.** When the Levites entered into the work of God from the age of thirty, it would take, at least, twenty years for them to complete their service and retire.

    All those that were numbered of the Levites, whom Moses and Aaron and the chief of Israel numbered, after their families, and after the house of their fathers, FROM THIRTY YEARS OLD AND UPWARD EVEN UNTO FIFTY YEARS OLD, every one that came to do the service of the ministry, and the service of the burden in the tabernacle of the congregation,

    Numbers 4:46-47

2. **"The Word of my patience" takes about twenty-five years because the Levites were to minister between the ages of twenty-five to fifty.**

    This is it that belongeth unto the Levites: from TWENTY AND FIVE YEARS OLD and upward they shall go in to wait upon the service of the tabernacle of the congregation: And from the age of FIFTY YEARS they shall cease waiting upon the service thereof, and shall serve no more:

    Numbers 8:24-25

CHAPTER 7

"The Word of My Patience" for Caleb: Forty-Five Years

And now, behold, the LORD hath kept me alive, as he said, these forty and five years, even since the LORD spake this word unto Moses, while the children of Israel wandered in the wilderness: and now, lo, I am this day fourscore and five years old.

Joshua 14:10

1. Caleb received the call of God when he was just forty years old.

FORTY YEARS OLD WAS I WHEN MOSES THE SERVANT OF THE LORD SENT ME from Kadeshbarnea to espy out the land; and I brought him word again as it was in mine heart.

Joshua 14:7

Caleb's call began to manifest when Moses sent him on his first mission to lead the spies who went to spy out the land. Being sent on a mission is often the beginning of a great call. Do not despise the opportunity to do something exciting or even dangerous when God calls you. It may be the beginning of a great and exciting call. You must not pull back from the exciting and thrilling aspects of ministry. What a great opportunity it was to become a spy! Who would have ever thought that someone as ordinary as you would become a spy for God?

2. Caleb entered The Promised Land with the people of God after wandering through the wilderness for forty long years.

And thou shalt remember all the way which THE LORD THY GOD LED THEE THESE FORTY YEARS IN THE WILDERNESS, to humble thee, and to prove thee, to know what was in thine heart, whether thou wouldest keep his commandments, or no. And he humbled thee, and suffered thee to hunger, and fed thee with manna, which thou knewest not, neither did thy fathers know; that he might make thee know that man doth not live by bread only, but by every word that proceedeth out of the mouth of the LORD doth man live. Thy raiment waxed not old upon thee, neither did thy foot swell, THESE FORTY YEARS.

Deuteronomy 8:2-4

This forty-year period would put Caleb's age at about eighty years when he actually crossed the Jordan into The Promised

Land. Indeed, Caleb's only surviving friend from that era was Joshua. Both Joshua and Caleb must have been around eighty years old when they came out of the wilderness.

Every call of God is a "Word of my patience". A "Word of my patience" is a Word that requires patience, tolerance, endurance, tenacity, survival mentality, calmness, broad-mindedness, open-mindedness and acceptance of many things in order to see the fruit at the end of the day. Patience is a very important aspect of your calling. It is those who have both faith and patience who inherit the promises. (Hebrews 6:12).

3. Caleb was in The Promised Land after roaming around in the wilderness for forty years.

Then the children of Judah came unto Joshua in Gilgal: and Caleb the son of Jephunneh the Kenezite said unto him, Thou knowest the thing that the Lord said unto Moses the man of God concerning me and thee in Kadeshbarnea. FORTY YEARS OLD WAS I WHEN MOSES THE SERVANT OF THE LORD SENT ME FROM KADESHBARNEA TO ESPY OUT THE LAND; and I brought him word again as it was in mine heart. Nevertheless my brethren that went up with me made the heart of the people melt: but I wholly followed the LORD my God. And Moses sware on that day, saying, Surely the land whereon thy feet have trodden shall be thine inheritance, and thy children's for ever, because thou hast wholly followed the LORD my God. AND NOW, BEHOLD, THE LORD HATH KEPT ME ALIVE, AS HE SAID, THESE FORTY AND FIVE YEARS, EVEN SINCE THE LORD SPAKE THIS WORD UNTO MOSES, WHILE THE CHILDREN OF ISRAEL WANDERED IN THE WILDERNESS: AND NOW, LO, I AM THIS DAY FOURSCORE AND FIVE YEARS OLD. As yet I am as strong this day as I was in the day that Moses sent me: as my strength was then, even so is my strength now, for war, both to go out, and to come in. Now therefore give me this mountain, whereof the Lord spake in that day; for thou heardest in that day how the Anakims were there, and that the cities were great and fenced: if so be the Lord will be with me, then I shall be able to drive them out, as the Lord said. And Joshua blessed him, and gave unto Caleb the son of Jephunneh Hebron for an inheritance.

Joshua 14:6-13

Caleb remembered that it was forty-five years since he had been sent as a spy. Being sent as a spy was his first step into real ministry. The scripture above shows that Caleb asked for an inheritance after roaming around in the wilderness for forty years and being in The Promised Land for five years, making a total of forty-five years since he was sent forth as a spy.

CHAPTER 8

"The Word of My Patience" For Joshua: Seventy Years

Forty years old was I when Moses the servant of the Lord sent me from Kadeshbarnea to espy out the land; and I brought him word again as it was in mine heart. Nevertheless my brethren that went up with me made the heart of the people melt: but I wholly followed the Lord my God. And Moses sware on that day, saying, Surely the land whereon thy feet have trodden shall be thine inheritance, and thy children's for ever, because thou hast wholly followed the Lord my God. AND NOW, BEHOLD, THE LORD HATH KEPT ME ALIVE, AS HE SAID, THESE FORTY AND FIVE YEARS, EVEN SINCE THE LORD SPAKE THIS WORD UNTO MOSES, WHILE THE CHILDREN OF ISRAEL WANDERED IN THE WILDERNESS: AND NOW, LO, I AM THIS DAY FOURSCORE AND FIVE YEARS OLD.

Joshua 14:7-10

And it came to pass after these things, that Joshua the son of Nun, the servant of the Lord, died, being an HUNDRED AND TEN YEARS OLD.

Joshua 24:29

1. **Joshua worked with Caleb for the forty-five years that they wandered through the wilderness and entered The Promised Land.**

   Forty years old was I when Moses the servant of the Lord sent me from Kadeshbarnea to espy out the land; and I brought him word again as it was in mine heart. Nevertheless my brethren that went up with me made the heart of the people melt: but I wholly followed the Lord my God. And Moses sware on that day, saying, Surely the land whereon thy feet have trodden shall be thine inheritance, and thy children's for ever, because thou hast wholly followed the Lord my God. AND NOW, BEHOLD, THE LORD HATH KEPT ME ALIVE, AS HE SAID, THESE FORTY AND FIVE YEARS, EVEN SINCE THE LORD SPAKE THIS WORD UNTO MOSES, WHILE THE CHILDREN OF ISRAEL WANDERED IN THE WILDERNESS: AND NOW, LO, I AM THIS DAY FOURSCORE AND FIVE YEARS OLD.

   Joshua 14:7-10

   From the testimony of Caleb who was forty years old when he entered the ministry and eighty-five years old when he was receiving his inheritance in The Promised Land, we can deduce the timeline of Joshua's ministry.

   If Joshua was of a similar age to Caleb, being a colleague of Caleb, we may assume that Joshua also entered The Promised Land when he was also around eighty years old, just like Caleb.

2. **Joshua lived to be one hundred and ten years old.**

   And it came to pass after these things, that Joshua the son of Nun, the servant of the Lord, died, being an HUNDRED AND TEN YEARS OLD.

   Joshua 24:29

   This means that Joshua wandered around in the wilderness for forty years and lived another thirty years dividing the land for his people. From the age of eighty to the age of one hundred and ten, Joshua led the people of God to share the land and possess their inheritance. His charge was very specific! The ministry of Joshua was to share land for the children of Israel.

Joshua's ministry actually lasted for about seventy years. The first forty years of his ministry was basically wandering around in the wilderness. The last thirty years was spent dividing the land and actually fulfilling his ministry of dividing up The Promised Land for the tribes of Israel.

After the death of Moses the servant of the Lord, the Lord said to Joshua son of Nun, Moses' aide: "Moses my servant is dead. Now then, you and all these people, get ready to cross the Jordan River into the land I am about to give to them—to the Israelites. I will give you every place where you set your foot, as I promised Moses. Your territory will extend from the desert to Lebanon, and from the great river, the Euphrates—all the Hittite country—to the Mediterranean Sea in the west. No one will be able to stand against you all the days of your life. As I was with Moses, so I will be with you; I will never leave you nor forsake you. Be strong and courageous, because YOU WILL LEAD THESE PEOPLE TO INHERIT THE LAND I SWORE TO THEIR ANCESTORS TO GIVE THEM.

Joshua 1:1-6 (NIV)

CHAPTER 9

"The Word of My Patience" For Apostle Paul: Thirty Years

Therefore, since through God's mercy we have this ministry, we do not lose heart.

2 Corinthians 4:1 (NIV)

There is no clear date as to when Apostle Paul was born but most authorities place his birth between the years 3 and 5 AD. It is estimated that Paul was anything between six years younger or older than Jesus.

Apostle Paul's conversion and call to ministry on the road to Damascus seems to have occurred between the years 33 and 36 AD. Paul was converted when he was a young man. Paul was a young man when he supervised the killing of Stephen. According to the Mishnah (the Mishnah is the oldest authoritative post-biblical collection of Jewish oral laws), a young man is someone who is thirty years old or younger.

But he, being full of the Holy Ghost, looked up stedfastly into heaven, and saw the glory of God, and Jesus standing on the right hand of God, And said, Behold, I see the heavens opened, and the Son of man standing on the right hand of God. Then they cried out with a loud voice, and stopped their ears, and ran upon him with one accord, AND CAST HIM OUT OF THE CITY, AND STONED HIM: AND THE WITNESSES LAID DOWN THEIR CLOTHES AT A YOUNG MAN'S FEET, WHOSE NAME WAS SAUL.

Acts 7:55-58

Apostle Paul's death seems to have occurred between the years AD 62 and AD 67. Paul described himself as an old man. In the first century, an old man was around sixty years of age.

Yet I prefer to appeal to you on the basis of love. IT IS AS NONE OTHER THAN PAUL—AN OLD MAN and now also a prisoner of Christ Jesus—"

Philemon 1:9 (NIV)

With this timeline, we see that Apostle Paul was about thirty years at the time of his conversion and about sixty years at the time of his death.

It is clear from this that Apostle Paul's great and momentous call lasted about thirty years. There is nothing like a short call.

Paul did not achieve much in two years. Paul did not achieve much in three years. Paul did not achieve much in ten years. Paul achieved much only after thirty years in ministry. That is why the call of God is called "the Word of my patience". It is a Word that requires a lot of patience, endurance, calmness and determination.

Apostle Paul was estimated to be about sixty years old when he died. By the standards of those days, he lived a long life. Apostle Paul was born in Tarsus around AD 3. He is estimated to have died between AD 62 and AD 67. This means he would have been about sixty years old.

By AD 64, Emperor Nero of the Roman Empire was aggressively persecuting and killing Christians. Nero blamed Christians for starting a fire that destroyed Rome in AD 64. Paul may have been one of the Christians who were falsely arrested and executed at the time. It is also possible that Paul was arrested a few years after that, chained in a dungeon and sentenced to death for his faith and efforts in advancing the course of Jesus Christ. Remember Paul's words to Timothy in which he describes his situation as being chained like a criminal:

For which I am suffering, bound with chains as a criminal. But the word of God is not bound!

2 Timothy 2:9 (ESV)

Paul had been called by God. But the call of God was a "Word of my patience". In other words, it is a Word that requires patience to see its fulfilment. "The Word of my patience" is a Word that needs patience to be able to obey it. If Paul did not have tolerance, patience, forbearance, he would not have been able to experience the fulfilment of his ministry.

According to the traditions of the church, Paul was beheaded in Rome. The exact circumstances of his trial and death were never written down. From scripture, we know that Paul spent his final days living in the deplorable conditions of a Roman prison, awaiting his execution.

When Apostle Paul was certain that he was going to die, he wrote to his most loyal disciple and said: "For I am already being poured out as a drink offering, and the time of my departure has come. I have fought the good fight, I have finished the race, I have kept the faith. Henceforth there is laid up for me the crown of righteousness, which the Lord, the righteous judge, will award to me on that day, and not only to me but also to all who have loved his appearing" (2 Timothy 4:6-8).

This was a heartrending message from a man who saw death all around him every day. He wrote these words, expecting never to say any other words. These were his last words and his declaration of faith. The *Foxes Book of Martyrs* records that Paul was led by Nero's soldiers "out of the city to the place of execution, where he, after his prayers made, gave his neck to the sword."

Apostle Paul had received a call where he would become a chosen vessel who would take the gospel to the Gentiles. This call resulted in him enduring brutal attacks, oppression and mistreatment. Paul suffered more than any other apostle. He reaped the persecution that he had released against the church. He was tormented by wicked men who did exactly what he used to do against the church.

And there was a certain disciple at Damascus, named Ananias; and to him said the Lord in a vision, Ananias. And he said, Behold, I am here, Lord. And the Lord said unto him, Arise, and go into the street which is called Straight, and enquire in the house of Judas for one called Saul, of Tarsus: for, behold, he prayeth, And hath seen in a vision a man named Ananias coming in, and putting his hand on him, that he might receive his sight. Then Ananias answered, Lord, I have heard by many of this man, how much evil he hath done to thy saints at Jerusalem: And here he hath authority from the chief priests to bind all that call on thy name. BUT THE LORD SAID UNTO HIM, GO THY WAY: FOR HE IS A CHOSEN VESSEL UNTO ME, TO BEAR MY NAME BEFORE THE GENTILES, AND KINGS, AND THE CHILDREN OF ISRAEL: FOR I WILL SHEW HIM HOW GREAT THINGS HE MUST SUFFER FOR MY NAME'S SAKE.

Acts 9:10-16

Paul was a determined man. He knew that he had received a call to ministry because he had received mercy (2 Corinthians 4:1).

CHAPTER 10

"The Word of My Patience" For Peter: Thirty Years

Because thou hast kept the word of my patience, ...

Revelation 3:10

T here is no evidence in the scripture for a specific age for any of the disciples. However, there are clues from the gospels as to the age of Apostle Peter and the other twelve disciples. There is also evidence from Jewish culture and from the Mishnah as to how old the disciples must have been when they started following Jesus. The Mishnah is the oldest authoritative post-biblical collection of Jewish oral laws that existed in the time of Jesus.

Let us have a look at what the Mishnah said about the time of Jesus. Indeed, it reveals a very regimented educational path for young boys in Judaism.

Realities from the Mishnah

At five years old a young man is fit for the Scripture.

At ten years, a young man is fit for the Mishnah (the oral Torah).

At thirteen years old a young man is fit for the fulfilling of the commandments.

At fifteen years, a young man is fit for the Talmud (making Rabbinic interpretations).

At eighteen years, a young man is fit for the bride-chamber.

At twenty years, a young man is fit for pursuing a vocation.

At thirty years, a young man is fit for authority (able to teach others).

As you can see from the above, almost all young Jewish men were married by the age of eighteen. Peter is the only disciple who is known to have been married. The Bible clearly makes mention of Peter's mother-in-law. "And when Jesus was come into Peter's house, he saw his wife's mother laid, and sick of a fever. And he touched her hand, and the fever left her: and she arose, and ministered unto them." (Matthew 8:14-15). No other disciple seemed to have had a mother-in-law or a wife. If this is the case, then most of the disciples may have been below the age of eighteen, with some as young as fifteen.

Also, at that time, education for the Jewish child concluded at the age of 15 - "At fifteen years, a young man is fit for the Talmud." Unlike today, where people want their children to become lawyers or doctors, Jews would desire their sons to be selected for training as Rabbis.

If you were fifteen years old and had completed your basic training in the Torah, most people would find a Rabbi to take them on as a student. For instance, Apostle Paul was a young Jewish student from Tarsus (Saul of Tarsus) who was sent by his rich parents to Jerusalem to study under a great Rabbi, Gamaliel. If your child did not qualify to be under such a great Rabbi, he was likely to become an apprentice in the family business.

We see that the disciples were apprentices with their fathers when they were called to the ministry. ("And so was also James, and John, the sons of Zebedee, which were partners with Simon. And Jesus said unto Simon, Fear not; from henceforth thou shalt catch men." - Luke 5:10). The realities we see in the Mishnah describe what is expected from a young man at each stage of his life. This means that the disciples were about twenty years old since "a young man is fit for a vocation at twenty years".

The disciples who were not married may have been less than eighteen years old because according to the Mishnah, at eighteen years a young man is fit for the bride-chamber. Since Peter was married, it is likely that he was also older than the other disciples. I would not put Peter's age as much higher than twenty because Andrew was also not married and brothers usually are in the same age group.

Because Jesus found them as apprentices in their family businesses, it is likely that none of them was considered as an outstanding Jewish scholarly student. This is why it was surprising to find people like James, John and Peter moving around with Jesus, a travelling Rabbi. "Now as they observed the confidence of Peter and John and understood that they were uneducated and untrained men, they were amazed, and began to recognize them as having been with Jesus." Acts 4:13 (NASB)

After the resurrection, the Chief Priests were shocked at their ability to speak, to teach and to preach because the disciples had clearly been unqualified for higher Rabbinic training, and that is why they had ended up as fishermen and apprentices.

Indeed, the Mishnah helps us to understand why Jesus did not begin his ministry until the age of thirty. It is only at the age of thirty that a man is fit for authority. No one would really be qualified for the authority of being a Rabbi until he was thirty, and no one would take on students until he was qualified to be a Rabbi at the age of thirty. So, Jesus Christ began His ministry at the very moment it was possible to begin; and when it was customarily appropriate to take on disciples and have students.

We also have a glimpse into the ages of Jesus and Peter when Jesus was asked to pay tax:

> When you take a head count of the Israelites to keep track of them, ALL MUST PAY AN ATONEMENT-TAX to God for their life at the time of being registered so that nothing bad will happen because of the registration. Everyone who gets counted is to give a half-shekel (using the standard Sanctuary shekel of a fifth of an ounce to the shekel) - a half-shekel offering to God. Everyone counted, age twenty and up, is to make the offering to God.
>
> Exodus 30:12-14 (MSG)

When Jesus was challenged about his tax paying, he sent Peter to the sea to catch a fish and use a coin to pay tax for Jesus Himself and Peter. Why did he not pay tax for the other disciples? He did not pay tax for the other disciples because they were not over twenty.

> And when they were come to Capernaum, they that received tribute money came to Peter, and said, Doth not your master pay tribute? He saith, Yes. And when he was come

into the house, Jesus prevented him, saying, what thinkest thou, Simon? Of whom do the kings of the earth take custom or tribute? Of their own children, or of strangers? Peter saith unto him, of strangers. Jesus saith unto him, then are the children free. NOTWITHSTANDING, LEST WE SHOULD OFFEND THEM, GO THOU TO THE SEA, AND CAST AN HOOK, AND TAKE UP THE FISH THAT FIRST COMETH UP; AND WHEN THOU HAST OPENED HIS MOUTH, THOU SHALT FIND A PIECE OF MONEY: THAT TAKE, AND GIVE UNTO THEM FOR ME AND THEE.

Matthew 17:24-27

I have said all these to show you that Peter started his ministry at about the age of twenty. We know that Peter died between AD 64 and AD 68. Peter received his calling from Jesus in his twenties. It took him well over thirty years to finish his calling. Every call is a "Word of my patience".

And I say also unto thee, That thou art Peter, and upon this rock I will build my church; and the gates of hell shall not prevail against it.

Matthew 16:18

From the time that Jesus spoke to Peter about his calling till the time that Peter died was over thirty years.

It is important that you understand the call of God. It is something that is going to require your patience. Many years will pass before you see the fruits of your calling coming to pass. It took Peter about thirty years to fulfil "the Word of my patience". Do not expect to fulfil your "Word of my patience" in two years!

CHAPTER 11

The Call of God: "The Word of My Patience"

And the God of all grace, WHO CALLED YOU to his eternal glory in Christ, after you have suffered a little while, will himself restore you and make you strong, firm and steadfast.

1 Peter 5:10

Dear brethren, I have tried to establish the fact that the call of God is always a "Word of my patience". It is time for you to rise up and go through what you must go through and bear the fruit you must bear.

1. **Receive the call to bear fruit.** Indeed, it is a call that needs patience. You need a lot of patience to bear the fruits God has called you to bear.

   Ye have not chosen me, but I have chosen you, and ordained you, that ye should go and bring forth fruit, and THAT YOUR FRUIT SHOULD REMAIN: that whatsoever ye shall ask of the Father in my name, he may give it you.

   John 15:16

2. **Receive the call to church growth.** You will need patience to help you go through the opposition you are going to face. If you will ever see church growth, you will have to be very patient.

   And it may be that I will abide, yea, and winter with you, that ye may bring me on my journey whithersoever I go. For I will not see you now by the way; but I trust to tarry a while with you, if the Lord permit.

   But I will tarry at Ephesus until Pentecost. For A GREAT DOOR AND EFFECTUAL IS OPENED UNTO ME, and there are many adversaries.

   1 Corinthians 16:6-9

3. **Receive the call to go to the uttermost parts of the world.** You need patience to fulfil this calling. If you will ever go to the ends of the world, you will have to be very patient.

   But ye shall receive power, after that the Holy Ghost is come upon you: and ye shall be witnesses unto me both in Jerusalem, and in all Judaea, and in Samaria, and unto the uttermost part of the earth.

   Acts 1:8

4. **Receive the call of God to experience suffering.** It is a call that requires patience! You will need patience to take up your cross and follow Jesus!

    And he said to them all, If any man will come after me, LET HIM DENY HIMSELF, AND TAKE UP HIS CROSS DAILY, and follow me.

    Luke 9:23

5. **Receive the Word of prophecy about your future.** Jeremiah received a call when he was still in his mother's womb. He needed a lot of patience to see the fulfilment of that calling.

    Then the word of the Lord came unto me, saying, Before I formed thee in the belly I knew thee; and before thou camest forth out of the womb I sanctified thee, and I ordained thee a prophet unto the nations.

    Jeremiah 1:4-5

6. **Receive "the Word of my patience" to live in expectation of the return of Jesus Christ.** It is a call that needs patience. You will need patience to live in expectation of the coming of the Lord.

    BE PATIENT therefore, brethren, UNTO THE COMING OF THE LORD. Behold, the husbandman waiteth for the precious fruit of the earth, and hath long patience for it, until he receive the early and latter rain.
    Be ye also patient; stablish your hearts: for the coming of the Lord draweth nigh.

    James 5:7-8

Conclusion

We also have the prophetic message that is completely reliable. Dear brethren, you will do well to pay attention to it, as to a light shining in a dark place, until the day dawns and the morning star rises in your hearts. (2 Peter 1:19) Be diligent and fulfil "the Word of my patience".

To the making of many books there is no end!